HOW TO GUIDE
GIRL SCOUT DAISIES THROUGH

WELCOME TO THE
DAISY
FLOWER GARDEN

IT'S YOUR WORLD—CHANGE IT! A LEADERSHIP JOURNEY

Girl Scouts of the USA

CHAIR, NATIONAL BOARD OF DIRECTORS	CHIEF EXECUTIVE OFFICER	EXECUTIVE VICE PRESIDENT, MISSION TO MARKET	VICE PRESIDENT, PROGRAM DEVELOPMENT
Patricia Diaz Dennis	Kathy Cloninger	Norma I. Barquet	Eileen Doyle

WRITTEN BY Laura J. Tuchman

CONTRIBUTORS: Melinda Howard Flores, Kate Gottlieb, Toi James, Maja Ninkovic, Kelly Chatman

ILLUSTRATED BY Jennifer Kalis

DESIGNED BY Parham Santana

First published in 2008 by Girl Scouts of the USA
420 Fifth Avenue, New York, NY 10018-2798
www.girlscouts.org

ISBN: 978-0-88441-710-1

Printed in Italy

2 3 4 5 6 7 8 9/16 15 14 13 12 11 10 09 08

Pages 41 and 64: Quotes from Vita Sackville-West reproduced with permission of Curtis Brown
Group Ltd, London, on behalf of the Estate of Vita Sackville-West.
© Vita Sackville-West 1939 and 1958.
Page 5: Quote from *Through the Garden Gate* by Elizabeth Lawrence, edited by Bill Neal. © 1990 by
William Neal. Published by the University of North Carolina Press. www.uncpress.unc.edu
"The Oak and the Rose" by Shel Silverstein © 1981 by Evil Eye Music, Inc. Used by permission of
HarperCollins Publishers.
"God's Garden" by Dorothy Frances Gurney available in the Poets' Corner at theotherpages.org
"Friendship's Flower" by Helen Rice Steiner used with permission of The Helen Rice Steiner
Foundation, Suite 2100, Atrium Two, 221 East Fourth Street, Cincinnati, Ohio 45202.
www.helensteinerrice.com
"Afternoon on a Hill" © 1917, 1945 by Edna St. Vincent Millay.

Outdoor play activities on pages 46–47 adapted from the *Daisy Girl Scout Activity Book* (GSUSA,
2000) and The Guide for Daisy Girl Scout Leaders (GSUSA, 1993).

Thanks to Trina Pilonero of Silver Heights Farm, Jeffersonville, N.Y.; and John Adams of Hudson
Valley Organic, Wawarsing, N.Y., for planting and growing tips.

CONTENTS

"Young girls are very impressionable . . . that they can have somebody to look up to makes a big difference."

—Marisol Cruz, volunteer, Miami, Florida

DIGGING INTO THE DAISY GARDEN

Girl Scouts begins planting the seeds of leadership with its youngest members, Girl Scout Daisies. In this first leadership journey, Daisies are the keepers of the Daisy Flower Garden, a storybook world grounded in the values of the Girl Scout Law.

Globally diverse and dedicated to stewardship of the land, the Daisy Flower Garden is a place of enduring leadership values. Through its colorful characters, Girl Scout Daisies learn—and learn to live by—the Girl Scout Law. Embracing this cornerstone of Girl Scouting is their first step to leadership.

"I invite you to enter . . . into the world of gardens—a world as old as . . . history . . . and as new as the latest contribution of science; a world of mystery, adventure and romance; a world of poetry and philosophy; a world of beauty . . ."

—Elizabeth Lawrence, American garden writer, 1903–1985, from *Through the Garden Gate*

The Garden Story and the Girl Scout Law

AMAZING DAISY AND HER FLOWER FRIENDS

Besides the three young girls, the garden story features 11 flowers and one golden honeybee. The central flower character is Amazing Daisy, who represents the entire Girl Scout Law. Being a daisy, she's a member of the world's largest flower family.

Three of Daisy's flower friends are also, botanically speaking, members of the same family. So in the story, they are Daisy's "cousins." Each flower friend represents one line—one value—of the Girl Scout Law.

I n the story of "Amazing Daisy and the Daisy Flower Garden," three young girls pass by a neglected community garden one afternoon and spot something bright among the weeds: a single white daisy. But this is no ordinary daisy. It is a flower that speaks to the girls and welcomes them to the garden that is the basis for this first Daisy leadership journey.

Each session of the journey features one chapter of the garden story, so a "Garden Story Time"—a reading and discussion period—is built into each session. With each chapter, girls take part in activities that parallel the story's action. For example, as the fictional characters improve their storybook garden, Girl Scout Daisies engage in their own planting or growing project. And at the end of the journey, they'll create a message for future Girl Scout Daisies, taking inspiration from the messages discovered and created in the story.

Sessions also include active "thinking" games and other activities related to the garden theme and Girl Scout values, history, and traditions. You'll use these games and activities to guide girls to learn more about themselves, their families, their world, and the Girl Scout Promise and Law.

Given the richness of the storybook garden, each journey session offers a variety of paths to explore. Depending on the time available and the girls' interest, you might pursue some of these in greater depth, perhaps even expanding a few into multiple sessions. The journey can then be enjoyed over a much longer period than the six sample sessions provided in this guide.

Making the Most of the Garden Story

Activities in each sample session of the journey build on the story's themes to teach girls the values of the Girl Scout Law. Storytelling sparks the imagination and builds a love and appreciation of language. So consider lining up some "guest readers"—teen or adult—to add flair to each Garden Story Time and really bring the story alive. Fun vocabulary pointers, called "Words for the Wise," are built into the girls' book, and these can be read to the girls, too.

The garden story offers many "teachable moments." Some are obvious, such as Marco being upset by Campbell's ball-playing skills, Campbell just smiling at the friendly teasing of her friend Viken, or all three girls venturing alone into a garden rather than walking straight home after school. Use these story scenes to point out important lessons to the girls, particularly those related to personal safety and self-confidence.

For example, use the Marco incident to let girls know they should not allow the jealousy of others to squash their talents. And use the girls falling asleep in the garden to point out the difference between a fairytale with talking flowers, where it's perfectly safe for little girls to lie down and take a nap, and the real world, where little girls are taught to go straight home after school and falling asleep alone outdoors is a no-no. Other teachable moments are more subtle. Many will depend on your region and how its assets (beekeepers, master gardeners, and other community members) match up with the garden story.

So have fun guiding the girls through these moments when you happen upon ones that interest you and your group of Daisies. Even the short activity about keys in the girls' book (page 31) is a teachable moment: It's fun to imagine magical keys that lead to secret treasures, and it's fun to have lots of keys—not just door keys but keys to diaries, treasure chests, and music boxes. But in real life, some keys are very private—they must always be kept out of reach of strangers.

WORKING WITH THE GIRLS' BOOK

The girls' book also follows a chapter-by-chapter design, and is sprinkled with "thinking" and creative activities. Use these as you like, according to the skills and abilities of your group of Daisies. Encourage girls to share their books with their families between sessions, and to revisit them at the start of sessions, as girls arrive and settle in.

Daisy's Flower Friends

The story's flower characters carry forward the colors and Girl Scout Law values of the Daisy Learning Petals, which were first introduced in 2000 to help Girl Scout Daisies learn the Promise and Law. This means that girls who have started to learn these colors and values will likely find the flowers a smooth and exciting transition. The flower friends expand upon the petals to create a global community that mirrors real flowers in the real world. So the Daisy Flower Garden is filled with fascinating flower facts. For example, spring green, the petal that represented being considerate and caring, is now the color of Zinni, the zinnia. This many-petaled flower, which traces its botanical origins to Mexico, is one the few flowers in the world to sport spring green blooms. Here's a quick guide to the 10 flower friends, their characteristics, and their Law values, in order of their appearance in the story:

Sunny, the sunflower, **is yellow. She's a cousin of Amazing Daisy from Great Britain and is friendly and helpful.**

Zinni, the zinnia, **is spring green. She's a cousin from Mexico and is considerate and caring.**

Mari, the marigold, **is orange. She's a cousin from Africa and has family in France, Central America, and Mexico. She represents being "responsible for what I say and do."**

Tula, the tulip, **is red and courageous and strong. She's from Holland but her family is originally from Iran.**

Lupe, the lupine (pronounced Loo-PAY), is light blue and honest and fair. She's from Texas and Minnesota, and likes to summer in Maine. She has family all around the world.

Gloria, the morning glory, is purple and represents "respect myself and others." She's from California and has family throughout South America and Asia.

Gerri, the geranium, is magenta and represents respecting authority. She grew up in the mountains of Virginia and has family all around the world, especially in Greece.

Clover is green and sports white flowers from time to time. She uses resources wisely: She offers food for bugs and animals, good-luck charms for people, and nectar for bees. Her family is from all over the world.

Vi, the violet, is violet in color and is "a sister to every Girl Scout." She's from Australia.

Rosie, the rose, who loves to look at the world through her rose-colored petals, likes to "make the world a better place." She's a native of America and has family in all 50 states.

Awards in the Daisy Garden

Like all Girl Scout journeys, this one focuses on the leadership philosophy of girls **discovering** (themselves and their values), **connecting** (caring and teaming), and **taking action** (to improve their communities and the world). For Girl Scout Daisies, the best way to experience this leadership philosophy is by practicing the Girl Scout Law. So the journey's three awards, which tie directly to the garden theme, recognize girls' progress in applying the Law to their lives.

Watering Can Award

This first award represents girls being "responsible for what I say and do." Girls earn the award by caring for their mini-garden and beginning to understand how the Promise and Law play out in their daily lives. The watering can, a source of nourishment in a garden, also serves as a dual symbol: The girls nurture their mini-garden while they nurture themselves by learning the Promise and Law. (Session 3 is an ideal time for girls to earn this award.)

Golden Honey Bee Award

This second award represents taking action—in a big or small way—to make the world a better place. The award is named for Honey, the bee who leads the girls of the garden story to Amazing Daisy and the Daisy Flower Garden. Girls earn the award as they complete a planting or growing project in their community (probably around Session 5).

Amazing Daisy Award

This final award represents knowing—and living—the Promise and Law, just like Amazing Daisy. (Girls receive it at a closing garden party celebration as they say the Promise and Law.)

The first two awards show the girls their progress and accomplishment along the journey, which culminates in the more important end goal: making the Promise to live by the Law. The sequence noted here for awards is just a suggestion. The experience you tailor with girls and their families will drive the awards sequence for your group of Daisies.

Sample Sessions at a Glance

SESSION 1

Welcome to the Daisy Flower Garden

Girls meet one another, hear about the Girl Scout Promise, sample the Daisy story, plant their mini-garden, and play Daisy Circle, Garden-Style.

SESSION 2

Buzzing Toward Girl Scout Values

Girls say hello in Spanish, recite the Girl Scout Promise, greet each other with the Girl Scout sign, water their mini-garden, and enjoy a "garden scamper"—all the while discovering how Girl Scout values are part of their daily lives.

SESSION 3

Greetings and Friendships

Girls say hello in French, deepen their understanding of the Girl Scout Law—particularly "being responsible for what I say and do"—maintain their mini-garden, and play an "imitating nature" game. Their achievements earn them the Watering Can Award.

WHAT IF A GIRL MISSES A SESSION?

Find a way for her to do something similar to what she missed so she can still move forward with her sister Daisies and earn her awards. If she misses a Garden Story Time and Discussion, for example, perhaps she can read the chapter with a family member or older friend. If she misses the team's planting or growing project time, she can take the lead in a follow-up step, such as talking with her team members and sharing what they learned.

SESSION 4

Good Thoughts, Good Deeds, Garden Needs

Girls say hello in Dutch and Persian/Farsi, maintain their mini-garden, brainstorm a larger planting/growing project, and play What's in the Bag—all the while deepening their understanding of how Girl Scout values play out in their lives and their community.

SESSION 5

Doing and Growing

Girls say hello in Japanese, maintain their mini-garden, plant/grow (according to their Take Action Project), and take part in an active Secret Garden Time. Girls who carry out their Take Action Project to make the world a better place earn the Golden Honey Bee Award.

SESSION 6

Celebrating the Law with a Garden Party

Girls say hello in a language of their choice, reflect on their Take Action Project, and say and explain the meaning of the Girl Scout Law. For their achievements, girls are awarded the Daisy Flower Award and rewarded with a garden party.

When girls miss a team meeting, your goal is to assist them in finding ways to have the same learning and growing opportunity—and to understand how they can contribute to the group. Girls may not have the exact same experience but they can each take away new insights, connections, and a sense of accomplishment.

Identifying Journey "Helpers"

The Daisy Friends and Family Network

Encourage family and friends—adults and teens—to join sessions to lead garden-related projects, lend a hand with garden-inspired snacks, or organize garden-themed outings (to public gardens, beekeepers, Girl Scout outdoor properties, etc.).

Think of these Network members as direction givers and informative signposts at each stop along the journey. This network of volunteers will prove extremely valuable in organizing an age-appropriate Take Action Project for your group of Daisies. Having their assistance in identifying project possibilities will help your group focus on what is practical and doable in your area in a way that allows girls to experience, perhaps for the first time, what it's like to make a positive impact on the environment.

Ask Network Members to Assist

Use the welcome letter and Friends and Family Checklist on the following pages to ask Network members to assist in creating a list of community garden assets: school gardens, city gardens, gardens at hospitals and nursing homes, Girl Scout properties, playgrounds, etc. The Project Possibilities section lets Network members divide assets into two categories: community areas that might benefit from simple beautification (a planting/growing gift, such as an indoor herb garden or easily maintained primrose plantings for a nursing home) and community areas that might benefit from more sustained care (such as gifts of compost or ladybugs for an established community garden).

In Session 4, after you read Chapter 4 of the garden story to the girls, use the Network's lists to start a discussion about how the Girl Scout Daisies might follow through on some of the needs voiced by the flower characters. Let the girls know that although they're young, they can still think about, and then help, a garden space in their community.

Worms and Ladybugs

Following the story line, two interesting and logical choices for a Take Action Project are worm composting and ladybug growing (see pages 62–63). Getting involved with dirt and bugs might sound like a bit much for a busy volunteer guiding a group of 5- and 6-year-olds, but these are simple projects. And they are highly beneficial gifts for a garden.

More important, your group of Daisies must decide what community space could use the kind of Take Action Project girls their age can do. That's where the Daisy Friends and Family Network and its brainstorming lists will prove invaluable.

The lists, which girls will take home to their families, give them a chance to talk about gardening hopes and plans with family members. In this way, Daisy families can offer their ideas and advice for turning the girls' garden plans into a true community action project. It's likely that some Daisy parents have gardening skills and/or knowledge—and time to join you as volunteers to make your group's project a community success. The welcome letter and Friends and Family Checklist are designed to identify and encourage that volunteerism.

> ### CITY, COUNTRY, AND SUBURBS, TOO
>
> Depending on your location, you might encourage your Network families to play tourist with their Daisies or serve as host to other Daisies and their families as time and circumstances allow. For example, an urban Daisy and her family could venture out to the suburbs or the country to visit gardens. Or a rural Daisy and her family could travel into the city to experience the wonders of urban gardens. In some areas, it may be possible for urban, suburban, and rural Daisy families to meet each other and "swap" their varied garden experiences.

"I began gardening with nasturtiums in my mother's discarded cold cream jars, and with sweet potatoes in a jar of water. And very satisfactory they were too. And are."

—Henry Mitchell, American garden writer, 1923–1993, from "A Garden in the City," 1988, in *Garden Dreams*

Welcome! Help Make Your Daisy's Experience Bloom with Possibilities

Dear Daisy Friends and Family Network:

Your Girl Scout Daisy has joined a team of girls on a unique journey into the Daisy Flower Garden. As the girls explore planting, growing, and the positive values of the Girl Scout Law, they will also get their first taste of environmental stewardship.

Your active participation can make the girls' experience even more valuable and memorable. Please take a moment to review the enclosed checklist to tell us which areas you might know something about (or be willing to learn), or have time to volunteer for, so that your Daisy and her sister Girl Scouts will have the richest experience possible.

Then please identify on the enclosed Garden Project Possibilities list any garden spaces in your community that might benefit from the Daisies' help. And if you have any community contacts who might like to assist, let us know that, too.

The girls and I look forward to hearing from you—and seeing you at sessions throughout the journey.

Sincerely,

[YOUR NAME]

DAISY FRIENDS AND FAMILY CHECKLIST

Please have your Daisy return this list to her next Daisy session.

● ●

☐ **YES, I WANT TO HELP THE DAISIES GROW.** I am ready and willing to volunteer my:

_____ Gardening knowledge

_____ Knowledge of beneficial garden insects (particularly ladybugs)

_____ Composting knowledge (especially worms)

_____ Time to bring snacks (especially nutritious ones!)

_____ Time as a driver (if needed for garden-themed outings or the Take Action Project)

_____ Crafts experience

_____ Time as an all-around Daisy leadership journey helper

My name: _____

My contact info: _____

_____

☐ **YES! I HAVE CONTACTS IN THE COMMUNITY WHO COULD HELP.** They are:

Name: _____

Contact info: _____

Name: _____

Contact info: _____

_____

☐ **YES! I KNOW OF GARDEN PROJECT POSSIBILITIES IN OUR COMMUNITY.**

Areas in my Daisy's community that might benefit from simple beautification (a planting/growing gift, such as an indoor herb garden or easily maintained primrose plantings; a garden cleanup day, etc.):

1. _____

2. _____

3. _____

4. _____

5. _____

Areas in my Daisy's community that might benefit from more sustained care (such as repeated "gifts" of compost for a community garden, or the release of ladybugs in a garden needing pest control):

1. _____

2. _____

3. _____

4. _____

5. _____

My name: _____

My contact info: _____

"My Daisy troop is in the delightful getting-to-know-you phase. These girls come with sunny personalities and are learning to work together."

—Anne-Marie Faul, Girl Scout volunteer, Katy, Texas

YOU AND YOUR GROUP OF GIRL SCOUT DAISIES

Throughout this journey, you and the girls will gain deeper knowledge of one another and the rich traditions of Girl Scouting. So take some time to understand the likes and needs of Daisy-age girls, and then dip into the history of Girl Scouts and the "what and how" of creating quality Girl Scout experiences.

As you read about the long-lasting leadership benefits of Girl Scouting, think about your own perspective on leadership. Your interest and enthusiasm are sure to be a driving force for the Daisies.

Understanding Daisy-Age Girls

Throughout this journey, your kindergarten and first-grade "gardeners" will expect you to understand who they are at their age. As Girl Scout Daisies move through kindergarten and/or turn 6, you might notice that they test your limits, recognize and acknowledge their mistakes, attempt new activities more easily, and get tired or lose interest faster.

Keep in mind that kindergarteners:

Need permission to move on from an activity (they often ask, "Can I . . . ?") and tend to focus on one thing at a time.	*So concentrate on one action at a time, and keep their expectations clear and simple.*
Like rules and routines, which they accept as unbendable.	*So they learn best through rituals, repetitive activities, and structured games. This means that repeating stories, poems, songs, and games will prove enjoyable for them.*
Want to explain things and have things explained to them, although they can be fidgety (kindergarteners often have trouble sitting still and listening).	*So offer lots of encouragement—kindergarteners need it in order to move on to the next activity.*
Need things explained in a very literal way—a phrase like "keep your eyes peeled" confuses them, and they don't understand complex logic the way adults do.	*So use lots of active exploration of concrete materials, such as garden objects, paints, or arts and crafts supplies.*
Need your understanding and patience in order to see the world from another point of view—they might think "my way" is the only way.	*So, when you can, include role-playing—at this age, it's an important form of self-expression.*
Enjoy doing things for themselves—the more they can do on their own, the more confidence they develop.	*So give girls some room to figure things out on their own. Ask them to predict what's going to happen in the garden story, for example, or ask them to look at the pictures in the story characters for clues to what the characters are like.*

"All the flowers of all the tomorrows are in the seeds of today."

—Indian proverb

Keep in mind that first-graders:

Approach the world logically in small ways for the first time; they are beginning to understand cause and effect in the natural world (for example, water makes grass grow).	*So be ready to explain the "why" of things.*
Begin to see and consider other points of view. First-graders want to help others and are ready for individual and group responsibility.	*So give girls space to do things for themselves and frequent opportunities to help others.*
Want to try everything, but might not be able to finish what they start.	*So provide lots of encouragement, and prepare yourself for a busy group, bustling with noise and activity.*
Prefer large-motor activities (easel painting or out-of-doors activities) to small motor activity (writing).	*So use games when you can for learning, and teach girls poems, riddles, and songs.*
Love jokes and guessing games, as well as artistic projects with concrete materials such as paints and clay.	*So take advantage of the art projects in this journey and make good use of paints, coloring, dancing, and singing when you can.*

What + How: Creating a Quality Experience

I t's not just what girls do, but how you engage them that creates a high-quality experience. All Girl Scout activities are built on three processes that make Girl Scouting unique from school and other extracurricular activities. When used together, these processes—Girl Led, Cooperative Learning, and Learning by Doing—ensure the quality and promote the fun and friendship so integral to Girl Scouting. Take some time to understand these processes and how to use them with Daisies.

Girl Led

"Girl led" is just what it sounds like—girls play an active part in figuring out the what, where, when, how, and why of their activities. So encourage them to lead the planning, decision-making, learning, and fun as much as possible. This ensures that girls are engaged in their learning and experience leadership opportunities as they prepare to become active participants in their local and global communities.

With Daisies, this might mean:

- Repeating an activity that girls say they really enjoyed

- Listening to their ideas on how to make activities even more fun

- Giving girls the opportunity to ask questions or predict what's going to happen next in the Daisy story

Learning by Doing

Learning by Doing, also known as Experiential Learning, is a hands-on learning process that engages girls in continuous cycles of action and reflection that result in deeper understanding of concepts and mastery of practical skills. As they participate in meaningful activities and then reflect on them, girls get to explore their own questions, discover answers, gain new skills, and share ideas and observations with others. Throughout the process, it's important for girls to be able to connect their experiences to their lives and apply what they have learned to their future experiences.

You'll see, for example, questions and discussion ideas after each chapter of the Daisy story, and suggestions for incorporating your own experiences with the values of the Girl Scout Law into the sessions. So give yourself and the girls permission for a little quiet time to think, talk, and reflect. Resist the urge to rush from "doing" to "more doing." Plenty of additional tips are woven throughout this guide, and the girls also have opportunities to reflect on their experiences in their book.

Cooperative Learning

Through cooperative learning, girls work together toward shared goals in an atmosphere of respect and collaboration that encourages the sharing of skills, knowledge, and learning. Working together in all-girl environments also encourages girls to feel powerful and emotionally and physically safe, and it allows them to experience a sense of belonging even in the most diverse groups.

With Daisies, you can try:

- Having older or more skilled girls lead others in the group (in a range of activities, from learning the Promise to tying a shoelace)

- Asking girls to work on projects together (a great way to practice the values in the Girl Scout Law)

- Asking girls to share and brainstorm ideas while gathering in a Daisy Circle

The First "Daisy"

Girl Scout Daisies might like knowing that their Girl Scout grade level is named for the founder of Girl Scouts, Juliette "Daisy" Gordon Low. Called "Daisy" by her family and friends, Low was well ahead of her time and known for her boldness and humor. She put no limits on girls' lives. Her nickname came from her uncle who, seeing her as a baby, said, "I'll bet she is going to be a 'Daisy!' "

The Girl Scout Law

Since its start, Girls Scouts has followed a set of values called the Girl Scout Law (or Laws). The original Laws were written in 1912. They were modified and updated in 1913, 1916, 1917, and 1920. A modern version of the Law was written in 1972 and the current Law was adopted in 1996.

Girl Scouts and the World

Girl Scouts of the USA is a member of the World Association of Girl Guides and Girl Scouts (WAGGGS), which was formed in 1928. Daisies can receive the World Trefoil Pin, which symbolizes that they are members of WAGGGS. The pin is often given to girls on World Thinking Day. Its placement—above the Girl Scout membership pin—helps Daisies understand that WAGGGS is larger than Girl Scouts of the USA.

Traditions: Something to Celebrate

Celebrating Girl Scout traditions connects Girl Scouts to one another, to their sister Girl Scouts and Girl Guides around the world, and to the generations of girls who were Girl Scouts before them. A few Girl Scout traditions are mentioned here and also woven into the journey sessions. The Daisy journey also includes a new "tradition"—Hello Around the World, which offers a great way for girls to begin seeing themselves as part of a worldwide sisterhood. Feel free to incorporate additional traditions into your sessions (your local Girl Scout council will have many worth sharing). And don't forget to involve the girls in creating and passing on new traditions—even silly songs, cheers, or simple expressions.

Girl Scout Sign

Girl Scouts make the Girl Scout sign when they say the Girl Scout Promise. The sign is formed by holding down the thumb and little finger on the right hand, leaving the three middle fingers extended (these three fingers represent the three parts of the Promise).

Girl Scout Handshake

The Girl Scout handshake is the way many Girl Guides and Girl Scouts greet one another. They shake their left hands while making the Girl Scout sign with their right hand. The left-handed handshake—in contrast to the standard American right-handed handshake—represents friendship, because the left hand is closer to the heart than the right.

Friendship Circle and Friendship Squeeze

The Friendship Circle is often formed at the end of meetings or campfires as a closing ceremony. Everyone gathers in a circle; each girl crosses her right arm over her left and then holds hands with the person on each side of her. Once everyone is silent, one girl starts the friendship squeeze by squeezing the hand of the person to her left. One by one, each girl passes on the squeeze until it travels clockwise around the full circle.

Health, Safety, and Well-Being

SAFETY-WISE

Keep this Girl Scout reference handy. It details the safety net provided for girls in Girl Scouting. Use it along with any additional information from your council to plan trips and outdoor activities, and to promote the well-being of the Daisies every time you get together. It will be particularly useful as the Daisies carry out their planting or growing project.

CONTACT INFO FOR YOUR GIRL SCOUT COUNCIL

Name: _____

Can help with: _____

Phone: _____

E-mail: _____

The emotional and physical safety and well-being of girls is of paramount importance in Girl Scouting. Look out for the safety of girls by following *Safety-Wise* when planning all gatherings and trips, and:

• Checking into any additional safety guidelines your Girl Scout council might have, based on local issues

• Talking to girls and their families about special needs or concerns

Welcoming Girls with Disabilities

Girl Scouting embraces girls with many different needs at all age levels, and is guided by a very specific and positive philosophy of inclusion that benefits all: Each girl is an equal and valued member of a group with typically developing peers.

As an adult volunteer, you have the chance to improve the way society views girls with disabilities. One way to start is with language. Your words have a huge impact on the process of inclusion. People-First Language puts the person before the disability.

SAY	INSTEAD OF
She has autism.	She's autistic.
She has an intellectual disability.	She's mentally retarded.
She has a learning disability.	The girl is learning-disabled.
She uses a wheelchair.	She is wheelchair-bound.
She has a disability.	She is handicapped.

Learn What a Girl Needs

Probably the most important thing you can do is to ask the individual girl, or her parents or guardians, what she needs to make her experience in Girl Scouts successful. If you are frank with the girl and her parents and make yourself accessible to them, it's likely they will respond in kind, creating a better experience for all.

It's important for all girls to be rewarded based on their best efforts—not on completion of a task. Give any girl the opportunity to do her best and she will. Sometimes that means changing a few rules or approaching an activity in a more creative way. Here are a few examples:

• Invite a girl to perform an activity after observing others doing it first.

• Ask the girls to come up with their own ideas for how to adapt some journey activities.

Often what counts most is staying flexible and varying your approach with the girls. For a list of online resources, visit www.girlscouts.org and search on "disability resources."

Snack Time, Garden-Style

Simple, healthful, garden-inspired snacks keep your group of Daisies focused on the journey's garden theme. So invite the Daisy Friends and Family Network to pitch in with creative snack ideas—and snack-making for each session. A suggestion or two is all they'll need to take the garden theme and run with it. For example, in any season, bite-size veggies (cherry tomatoes, baby tomatillos, baby carrots) or vegetable sticks (carrot, celery, pepper—green, red, or yellow) and a simple yogurt dip make a great snack. And consider serving fresh juices in warmer months. Cold watermelon juice makes a refreshing break—and avoids the usual watermelon mess of rinds and seeds. Ahead of the session, a family member could simply cut a watermelon into chunks and run them through a blender. Then just chill the juice in a cooler or serving pitcher. At snack time, shake it up and serve it in small cups. Also, ask Daisy families to keep in mind that packaged sweets (cupcakes, donuts, cookies), though easy to find and easy to serve, won't teach the girls about gardening—or healthful eating. And a sugary snack may leave you with a group of girls on a sugar high followed by a sugar low.

Understanding the Journey's Leadership Benefits

Though filled with fun and friendship, this Daisy journey is designed to develop the skills and values young girls need to be leaders in their own lives and as they grow.

Girl Scouts of the USA has identified 15 national outcomes, or benefits, of the Girl Scout Leadership Experience. Activities in this Daisy journey are designed to enable kindergarten and first-grade girls to achieve seven of these outcomes, as detailed in the chart on the next page. You can notice the "signs" of these benefits throughout the journey.

Each girl is different, so don't expect them all to exhibit the same signs to indicate what they are learning along the journey. What matters is that you are guiding the Daisies toward leadership skills and qualities they can use right now—and all their lives.

For definitions of the outcomes and the signs that Girl Scout Daisies are achieving them, see the chart on the next page or *Transforming Leadership: Focusing on Outcomes of the New Girl Scout Leadership Experience* (GSUSA, 2008). Keep in mind, too, that the intended benefits to girls are the cumulative result of traveling through an entire journey—and everything else girls experience in Girl Scouting.

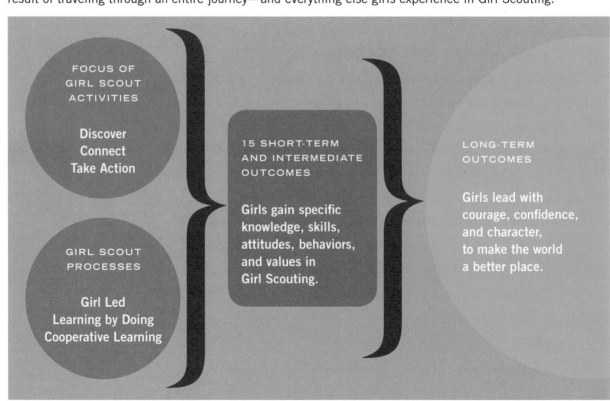

FOCUS OF GIRL SCOUT ACTIVITIES

**Discover
Connect
Take Action**

GIRL SCOUT PROCESSES

**Girl Led
Learning by Doing
Cooperative Learning**

15 SHORT-TERM AND INTERMEDIATE OUTCOMES

Girls gain specific knowledge, skills, attitudes, behaviors, and values in Girl Scouting.

LONG-TERM OUTCOMES

Girls lead with courage, confidence, and character, to make the world a better place.

NATIONAL LEADERSHIP OUTCOMES

		AT THE DAISY LEVEL, girls...	RELATED ACTIVITIES	SAMPLE "SIGN" When the outcome is achieved, girls might...
DISCOVER	**Girls develop a strong sense of self.**	are better able to recognize their strengths and abilities.	Sharing in the Daisy Circle and Garden Story Time discussions	make positive statements about their abilities or demonstrate to others what they can do (e.g., "I was a good friend to Luna today").
	Girls develop positive values.	begin to understand the values inherent in the Girl Scout Promise and Law.	Garden Story Time (all sessions)	identify actions that are fair/ unfair, honest/dishonest in various scenarios.
		recognize that their choices of actions or words have an effect on others and the environment.	Garden Story Time and the Take Action Project	give an example of when their actions made something better for someone else.
	Girls gain practical life skills— girls practice healthy living.	gain greater knowledge of what is healthy for mind and body.	Healthful snacks learned through the garden story	name behaviors that contribute to good health (e.g., eating fruit, getting exercise).
CONNECT	**Girls promote cooperation and team-building.**	begin to learn how to work well with others.	Mini-garden planting (begins in Session 1 and continues throughout)	name something about themselves that helps them work well in a group (e.g., "I listen well").
	Girls feel connected to their communities, locally and globally.	are better able to identify people and places that make up their community and understand their various contributions.	Take Action Project (Sessions 5 and 6)	identify people who provide services in their communities (e.g., doctors provide medical care, teachers provide education).
TAKE ACTION	**Girls can identify community needs.**	gain increased knowledge of their communities' assets.	Take Action Project brainstorming	name people/places they consider helpful and valuable in their communities.
	Girls educate and inspire others to act.	are better able to assist peers and seek help from them.	Take Action Project and Garden Party Celebration	respond to requests for help/ assistance with actions or words.

Your Perspective on Leadership

The Girl Scout Leadership philosophy—Discover + Connect + Take Action—implies that leadership happens from the inside out. As the Daisy journey evolves, the girls will discover, connect, and take action as leaders in their own right, and your thoughts, enthusiasm, and approach will be a key influence on them. So take some time to reflect on your own perspective on leadership.

Take a few minutes now—and throughout the journey—to apply Girl Scouts' three keys of leadership to yourself.

Discover **+** Connect **+** Take Action **=** Leadership

DISCOVER

When you read the Girl Scout Law, which line—and which flower character—means the most to you?

_____

_____

_____

How can you convey that to the Daisies?

_____

_____

_____

CONNECT

Can you recall a great experience you had that involved caring for something in the natural world, whether through gardening, helping with a community cleanup, or some other beautification or environmental effort?

_____

_____

_____

_____

TAKE ACTION

Why did you choose to volunteer with Girl Scouts?

_____

_____

_____

_____

How is Taking Action with the Daisies meaningful for you?

_____

_____

_____

_____

How does your volunteerism contribute to making the world a better place?

_____

_____

_____

_____

"**I like guiding Daisies** because they are virtual sponges and innocently open to new things. Most want to make new friends and experience the world."

—Angela Soden, Girl Scout volunteer and alumna, Blaine, Minnesota

THE JOURNEY'S 6 SAMPLE SESSIONS

Each session begins with a five-minute intro/welcome/ opening ceremony, and then features a 15-20-minute Garden Story Time and discussion, a 15-minute active activity, a 10-minute snack time (optional), and a 5-minute closing ceremony. Most sessions also include mini-garden watering time or planting project time.

If you like, vary the order of the reading/discussion and active activities from session to session. Each session runs roughly 60 minutes, but all times are just suggestions. You don't have to squeeze or stretch activities to fit a particular time. Everything can be adjusted to match the needs and desires of your group of Girl Scout Daisies.

But do aim to read through each session ahead of time. You'll then know of any needed materials or special preparations. Picturing each session as a whole will also help you bring it to life for the girls.

SAMPLE SESSION 1
Welcome to the Daisy Flower Garden

AT A GLANCE

Goal: Girls get to know one another, learn basic Girl Scout values, sample the Daisy story, and begin to plant/grow—all the while developing their ability to see that throughout the world, people (and plants) have unique identities.

- Opening Ceremony: Daisy Circle
- Girl Scout Promise
- Garden Story Time
- First Planting: a Mini-Garden
- Daisy Circle, Garden-Style (active time)
- Snack Time, Garden-Style (optional)
- Closing Ceremony: Friendship Squeeze

MATERIALS

- Girls' book and this guide
- Photocopies of the "COLOR ME" pages (8, 10, and 12) from the girls' book
- Colored pens/pencils/crayons
- Large easel paper or whiteboard/chalkboard
- Basil seeds (sweet basil or another sweet variety, such as Genovese) and/or seeds for leaf lettuce or greens (arugula, mizuna, Japanese red mustard), enough for each pair of girls
- Citrus seeds (oranges, grapefruits) if basil/lettuce seeds cannot be obtained (separate and label seeds if using various kinds)
- Lightweight gardening container, any shape, large enough to grow plants for each pair of girls, with drainage holes
- Potting mix, preferably a light mix that includes peat moss (enough for chosen container)
- Cup for scooping soil (plastic laundry cup or plastic/paper cup; anything easily handled by the girls)
- Wood craft sticks, Popsicle sticks, or plastic plant markers (one for every two girls) and marking pen
- Small, lightweight watering can (easily handled by girls) and water
- Map or globe of the world, or city/county map of your area (optional; see Map It Out on page 38)
- Snack (optional; see Snack Time, Garden-Style, page 27)

ADVANCE PREP

Write the Girl Scout Promise on a whiteboard or chalkboard, if available, or a large sheet of paper that can hang on the wall.

Have gardening container, soil, seeds, scooping cup, and watering can laid out on a table or easily in reach.

Decide on a safe, sunny spot to keep the girls' mini-garden between sessions—a place where it can be watched and watered by you, another volunteer, or an older Girl Scout acting as a Daisy "garden assistant." Carrying the "garden" to and from each session may be your best option—just use a container that's lightweight and easily portable.

AS GIRLS ARRIVE

Greet them and introduce yourself. Invite girls to sit together with their Daisy books (or photocopies of the "COLOR ME" pages that you give them) and have fun with the available crayons, colored pens/pencils, etc., until all the girls arrive.

Opening Ceremony: Daisy Circle

Once all girls arrive, gather them into a circle and explain that they are now in a Daisy Circle, something they will form to mark special times such as:

• Starting their Girl Scout time together

• Welcoming new girls and special visitors

• Sharing ideas

• Making group decisions

• Listening to the Daisy Flower Garden story

• Any other times they want to talk as a group

Next, explain that the girls will celebrate their Daisy Circle by saying hello and introducing themselves one by one by saying their name and one thing about themselves that they want all the girls to know. Start by example, saying something like, "Hi, my name is Ana and I love to dance!" The girls may need prompting, so be ready to ask questions like, "What is your favorite color? What games do you like to play?"

After the introductions, let the girls know how great it is that they are getting to know one another. Explain that they will share more about themselves each time they meet. Next, let the girls know it's now time to hear an important part of Girl Scouting.

VISUAL CLUES COUNT

For Daisies, who are beginning readers, visual cues are extremely important. Seeing the Girl Scout Promise written on a whiteboard or poster board, with three of the lines stacked under each other—and you pointing to each line as you say it—will help even the youngest members of your group understand that the Promise lists the three things Girl Scouts try:

TO SERVE GOD AND MY COUNTRY,
TO HELP PEOPLE AT ALL TIMES,
AND TO LIVE BY THE GIRL SCOUT LAW.

The same will be true of the Girl Scout Law and its 10 values. The large-scale "Amazing Daisy, Her Flower Friends, and the Girl Scout Law" poster included in this guide can serve as a colorful addition to your own large version of the Girl Scout Law written on poster board or a whiteboard/blackboard.

Girl Scout Promise

With the girls still in their Daisy Circle, explain that you are going to say the Girl Scout Promise, which is shared by all Girl Scouts. Explain that the Promise (which you have written on a whiteboard/chalkboard or large sheet of paper) is the way Girl Scouts agree to act toward one another and other people. After you read the full Promise, read it again, line by line, and ask the girls to repeat each line after you:

> *On my honor, I will try:*
> *To serve God and my country,*
> *To help people at all times,*
> *And to live by the Girl Scout Law.*

Once all four lines are said, ask the girls to say the whole Promise again, together with you. Explain to any first-year Daisies that they are starting to know an important part of Girl Scouting on their very first day as Girl Scout Daisies. And congratulate any second-year Daisies who already know the Promise. Let all the girls know that they will say the Promise together as a team each time they meet.

Next, talk to the girls about the last line of the Promise, which mentions the Law:

- Explain that the Girl Scout Law spells out all the good ways that Girl Scouts try to treat one another and the world—being kind and considerate, and friendly and helpful, caring and thoughtful.

- Explain that the Law is an important part of Girl Scouting that they'll learn throughout their time as Girl Scout Daisies.

- Emphasize that they'll learn all about the Law in the story of "Amazing Daisy and the Daisy Flower Garden," which you will now begin to read to them.

LET SECOND-YEAR DAISIES TAKE THE LEAD

If your group includes second-year Daisies, ask them if they would recite the Girl Scout Promise together as a way of teaching it to younger girls in the group. Or have them say one line of the Promise and let first-year Daisies follow with the next line.

Garden Story and Planting Tips

Going Global: An Option for a Future Session

The Daisy story features characters from around the world, so it's a good springboard for exploring other cultures. Invite a teen or adult who grew up in another country to speak to your group of girls. Ask your visitor to tell the girls about her childhood: the games she played, what her school was like, what foods she ate. Perhaps she can even teach the girls a few words of her native language.

If you can't find someone born in another country, invite someone from another region. Ask her to tell the girls about the weather there, the food, the landscape. Guide the girls to see that differences are what make people—and plants— unique and interesting, and that differences, as well as similarities, are to be respected and appreciated.

MAP IT OUT

If your group of Daisies includes girls born in various countries, states, or towns, consider hanging a world/city/county map on the wall and marking, with pushpins or sticky notes, where each girl is from. If girls come from a variety of countries, a globe would work well, too.

CITY DWELLERS: DON'T DESPAIR!

Even the most congested cities are home to community, courtyard, and rooftop gardens. If some Daisies haven't yet seen a garden, the ones in their area are likely well hidden. Garden-savvy parents among your Daisy families may be able to arrange a garden visit. Or check with your area's parks and planning offices to locate a garden near you. Owners of city gardens, even private ones, often enjoy showing their green spaces to visitors. Perhaps a few volunteers might guide a side trip to a community or rooftop garden—or to a farmers' market where the girls can meet some growers (and perhaps receive an invitation to visit the garden where their plants or flowers grew up). The American Community Gardening Association, in Columbus, Ohio, has started a database of community gardens—visit www.communitygarden.org or e-mail info@communitygarden.org.

The Mini-Garden: Keep It Lightweight and Worry-Free

This session marks the start of the girls' teaming up to plant a mini-garden. If being the keeper of the girls' mini-garden seems even the least bit overwhelming, keep in mind that a garden can be as simple and lightweight as seeds planted in a plastic bedding six-pack. Pairs or even groups of three to four girls can be assigned to one section of the six-pack, so that one lightweight container can accommodate as many as 24 girls. A bedding six-pack will guarantee a lightweight and easily portable garden—something volunteers who take public transportation to their meetings with Daisies will appreciate. A bedding six-pack also separates the plantings for easy identification while still keeping them together.

Using Resources Wisely

Large numbers of bedding six-packs are routinely used, and discarded, by growers. So inquiring at a local gardening center may land you recycled six-packs at no cost—a good lesson in using resources wisely, and living the Girl Scout Law!

If you're still queasy about maintaining a team garden, you may be tempted to give each girl a paper cup so she can plant her own mini-garden and carry it home. Wipe that thought from your mind! This journey isn't about individual botany experiments—it's about teamwork and understanding that a garden is the coming together of many elements. That's why the story of "Amazing Daisy and the Daisy Flower Garden" isn't a story of just one flower; it's about 11 flowers all living together in harmony.

WHY BASIL, LEAF LETTUCE, AND GREENS?

No matter where you live, your group of Daisies can easily grow basil, leaf lettuce, or mixed greens indoors any time of year. Basil simply requires good light and a temperature of 72 degrees or higher. Basil must also be watered lightly—let the soil get fairly dry and then use only warm water. Basil seeds will sprout in about 10 days. Greens and lettuce can sprout as quickly as overnight (especially if covered only lightly with potting mix or just peat moss). Greens, which can be sown thickly, will in record time offer a carpet of incredibly vivid color—a visual treat for the Daisies. Check with a local gardener if you believe your location has unusual needs.

Garden Story Time

Introduce the girl characters in the Daisy story by reading the short bios of each one, pausing at the end of each to ask a question or two to spark the girls' thinking. (Story-related questions are featured in the girls' book and in various Story Time tips in this guide—but feel free to ask your own.)

Aim to engage all the girls in the discussion. You might first read a question and offer an answer of your own. Say something like, "In this story, the girls live near an old garden. Let's think about where we live. I'll start. I live in an apartment on Spring Street, just two blocks from the train station." Then say something like, "Now let's go around our Daisy Circle so each of you can share an answer to this question. Maria, let's start with you. Where do you live?" If a girl doesn't have an answer, move the conversation along with some helpful prompts. Or switch to a new question; say something like, "Where is your favorite place to play outdoors?" After the girl answers, offer a positive comment, such as: "Thank you, Maria. How nice that you _____."

When all the girls have answered, recap what they've done:

• Let them know they've all just shared something special about themselves, such as where they live or where they like to play.

• Encourage them to write or draw their responses in their book and to share their book with their families.

• Remind them that they will share more about themselves at future Girl Scout sessions.

Then, let the girls know you will now read them the first chapter of the Daisy story.

After the reading, ask the girls the garden-related questions that follow Chapter 1 of the story:

• *Do you have a garden at home or near where you live? What makes it special?*

Explain to the girls that not everyone has a garden. Some people live in apartments and might not have room for a garden. Instead, they might have a window box or a pot of flowers.

Have the girls look at all the flowers, plants, animals, birds, and insects pictured in their books. Ask them: *If you could have any kind of garden you wanted, what would be in it?* Move around the Daisy Circle and invite all the girls to say what they might want in their garden. Let them know that they will have a chance to create their own garden right in their books.

TURN UP THE DRAMA

If you find girls eager for a chance to act out scenes from the garden tale, extend the Garden Story Time into drama. Giving the Daisies time to tell a few stories of their own helps them develop the ability to think things out in their own minds—a great leadership skill in itself.

"The tiniest garden is often the loveliest."

—Vita Sackville-West, poet, novelist, and gardener, 1892–1962, from *A Joy of Gardening*

First Planting: A Mini-Garden

Next, talk to the girls about how much fun it would be for them to create their own garden.

- Explain that you've brought some seeds for them to plant.

- Show the seeds and explain what kind they are, and perhaps ask the girls if they've ever eaten the foods that grow from them.

- Then ask the girls to form pairs to choose some seeds to plant together. (If using just one kind of seed, still let each pair choose a seed from the full batch. This will give the girls a sense of ownership—they chose what to plant.) Also, give each pair of girls a craft or Popsicle stick, or a plant marker.

- Explain to the girls that they will plant their seeds in one big pot—this gives the sense of planting a garden together. Later, as the seeds sprout and the plants grow, you can decide together whether transplanting is needed.

- Next, explain that the girls will label their plantings so they can remember who planted what. (If the girls can write their names, have them do so on the stick/marker. Otherwise, you can write the girls' names for them.)

- Have the girls involved in the full planting process. First ask them to take turns placing cupfuls of soil in the gardening container; continue until the container is sufficiently full for planting seeds.

- Next, have each pair of girls plant seeds in the potting mix—no more than perhaps a quarter of an inch from the surface of the soil. (A good rule of thumb is to place a seed no deeper in the soil than twice its height.) After the seeds are planted, have the girls mark their planting by placing their stick/marker in the soil by their seeds.

- Then have each pair of girls water their seeds (if planting basil, use warm water). Explain how watering a plant is like feeding it; water helps the plant grow.

WHAT'S A SEED?

Take a few minutes to guide the girls through some basics of what seeds are. Let them know that seeds are the way plants spread themselves around the Earth. Seeds get carried by the wind, by animals and people, by water, or by being pushed into the ground. Seeds basically hold tiny plants and food inside them, and are just waiting for a chance to sprout.

Seeds come in all shapes, textures, and sizes—from fluffy dandelion seeds to spiky pinecones, and from the tiniest speck of an orchid seed to giant palm tree seeds that look like double coconuts and can weigh as much as 50 pounds.

Ask the girls to name some seeds they've seen, such as the seeds of watermelons, oranges, and cherries. Have they ever seen the seeds of a maple tree, and how they fall to the ground like tiny whirlybirds twirling in the wind?

As the watering continues, ask the girls if any of them have ever helped their family water plants at home. If yes, ask them to share with the group what they've watered.

When all the girls have finished watering, explain that the container will now be placed in a warm, sunny location (usually by a window). And let them know that plants, like people, need time to grow. Their seeds need time—possibly just a day or two for greens and lettuce, 10 days for basil, as long as three-to-four weeks for citrus—to sprout. So at each future Girl Scout session, each pair of girls will water (lightly) its part of the pot and watch for growth. Explain that between sessions, you (or an assistant) will be the keeper of this mini-garden, watering it as needed.

GREEN THUMB? HAVE NO FEAR

Whether your home base is urban, suburban, or rural, gardening advice is just a phone call or e-mail away. Neighborhood gardeners and gardening stores are great resources, and state universities have extension services with volunteer "master gardeners" who serve the community. If you have Internet access, search on your state name and the words "agricultural extension" or "cooperative extension" to find a master gardener near you. The Web site of the National Gardening Association, www.garden.org, also offers a wealth of information, including specific advice about gardening with children.

"I have great faith in a seed. Convince me that you have a seed there, and I am prepared to expect wonders."

—Henry David Thoreau, writer and poet-naturalist, 1817–1862

WHAT IFS: AVOIDING A GARDEN "NO-SHOW" AND OTHER GARDEN "DISASTERS"

As the girls plant their mini-garden, keep an eye on the room temperature. At 72 degrees, which is ideal for germination, you needn't worry that nothing will sprout. If you're concerned that Daisies will have trouble handling tiny seeds, take the tried-and-true beans, peas, corn, or marigold approach to children's gardening. Seeds for these garden standards are larger than lettuce and basil seeds, and are known to be super sprouters. All four can also be grown indoors. You just won't have the easy picking of lettuce or the pleasing fragrance of basil (marigolds will tie nicely to the garden story, though) and, in the long run, a potted cornstalk may not be the most practical.

Daisy Circle, Garden-Style

The following game lets girls move about—and get the wiggles out—while furthering their understanding of gardens.

Gather the girls in a circle and explain to them that no matter where people live—house or apartment, city, suburb, or rural area—gardens are rarely far away. Talk about the gardens that your group of Daisies may know about—a flower patch at their school, a garden within a city park, a community garden in their neighborhood.

Explain to the girls that they'll now play a game where they will be the critters that live in a garden.

1. Start off by talking about four or five garden critters common to your community. If you live in an urban area and the girls have not had a chance to visit many gardens, likely they will have seen pigeons, small birds like sparrows, and possibly squirrels. Ask the girls if they know, for example, what sound a bird makes (a chirp) and how it moves about (by flapping its wings). Encourage the girls to name some critters on their own by saying something like, "Do you know any other garden critters in our area?" In this way, the girls will have a variety of critter sounds and movements in mind before the game starts.

2. Next, explain that you will call out the name of a garden critter, and all the girls, together, will pretend to be that critter in sound and movement.

3. The girls will continue the critter's sound/movement until you call out a new critter. Example: You call out "bird" and all the girls chirp and flap their arms. Then you call out "frog" and the girls jump up and down and say, "ribbit, ribbit." Once the activity gets going and the girls have moved through a few garden critters, consider asking the girls to take turns calling out critter names. You can then join the rest of the girls in making critter sounds and movements.

Closing Ceremony: Friendship Squeeze

Ask the girls to join together again in a Daisy Circle. Explain that they will now join hands for a special Girl Scout closing to their Girl Scout time together: the Friendship Circle and friendship squeeze. Let them know that adults call this kind of thing a closing ceremony. Explain that the word "ceremony" means celebrating something in a special way—so they are closing their time together today as Girl Scouts in a special way.

Explain that in a Friendship Circle, everyone gathers in a circle where they cross their right arm over their left in front of them and hold hands with the girls on either side. Once everyone is silent, one girl starts the friendship squeeze by squeezing the hand of the person to her left. One by one, moving clockwise, each girl passes on the squeeze until it travels all the way around the circle.

Let the girls know that they can end all their meetings with a friendship squeeze or they can think up their own ceremonies to perform. Keep in mind that it may prove challenging for the Daisies to suggest their own ceremonies. That's OK, because at their age, repeating a closing ceremony from meeting to meeting will be a welcome tradition.

Finally, thank the girls for a great first Girl Scout Daisy gathering. Encourage them to share their book with their families and to try their hand at creating their own special garden in their book's garden pages. And let them know that you really look forward to their next time together.

GREAT GARDENS TAKE TIME

Throughout this journey, as time allows, encourage the girls to engage in the "What's in Your Garden" art activity featured in their book. Suggest that they take their time "planting" their garden, and share the activity with their families at home between sessions. Encourage the girls to look at real gardens at home and in their neighborhood, as well as pictures of gardens in books, magazines, and newspapers. Let them know that they can use anything they like (colored pens, crayons, watercolor pencils, dried leaves or flowers) to create their garden. And they can take their time building their garden little by little. After all, real gardens require patience.

"Gardening is the art that uses flowers and plants as paint, and the soil and sky as canvas."

—Elizabeth Murray, American artist, author, and gardener, from *Monet's Passion: Ideas, Inspiration and Insights from the Painter's Gardens*

Tips for Outdoor Play

Outdoor play offers a natural learning environment and can serve as an extension of the journey's indoor garden-related activities. Feel free to offer some outdoor play whenever time and the weather permit. Be sure to check *Safety-Wise* for appropriate safety guidelines.

Outdoor Sights

This guided group activity requires nothing but observant eyes.

- Find an outdoor space big enough to move around in.

- Everyone lies on her back and looks up. What do you see?

- Next, everyone lies on her stomach and looks down. Now what do you see?

- Next, everyone crawls on the ground and looks at everything from an animal's point of view.

- Next, everyone looks for colors and shapes in nature. What kinds of things can you find?

You might also use some outdoor time to focus on seeds. On a hike or a simple walk, how many types of seeds can the girls find?

Outdoor Feeling

This activity heightens the sense of touch. Find an outdoor space offering varied textures: trees, grass, rocks, etc.

- Ask girls to touch several outdoor objects such as bark, leaves, soil, and stones to feel their textures. How would they describe them?

- Ask girls to stand in the shade, then in the sun. How does each feel?

- If there is a breeze or wind, have girls stand facing it for a few seconds. How does it feel? Now have the girls turn away from the wind. What feels different?

Outdoor Smells

This activity heightens the sense of smell. Find an outdoor space large enough for plenty of movement.

Ask the girls to breathe deeply. Then ask:

• What do you smell?

• Can you smell flowers, trees, water, animals?

• Do you smell anything unusual? Can you follow the scent to see what it is?

• Choose a small object, like a leaf, and pinch it. How does it smell?

For Daisies Who Know Their ABCs

Toward the end of first grade, when the girls are comfortable with the alphabet, an Alphabet Hike offers some outdoor fun: On a nature hike or walk around the neighborhood, girls are asked to look around them to find a natural object that begins with the letter A. When they find it, they call it out. Then the rest of the girls look for something that begins with B, and so on through the alphabet, or until all the girls have had the chance to name an object.

> "[She] who cultivates a garden,
> and brings to perfection flowers and fruits,
> cultivates and advances at the same time
> [her] own nature."
>
> —Ezra Weston, addressing the annual meeting of the Massachusetts Horticultural Society, 1836

SAMPLE SESSION 2
Buzzing Toward Girl Scout Values

AT A GLANCE

Goal: Girls discover how Girl Scout values are part of their daily lives.

- Opening Ceremony: Hello Around the World (Mexico and Spain) and the Girl Scout Promise
- Learning the Girl Scout Sign
- Mini-Garden Watering Time
- Garden Story Time

- Garden Scamper
- Snack Time (optional)
- Closing Ceremony: Friendship Squeeze

MATERIALS

- Girls' book and this guide
- Poster board with Girl Scout Promise (from Session 1) or Promise written on whiteboard/chalkboard
- Poster board with Girl Scout Law or Law written on whiteboard/chalkboard

- The girls' mini-garden
- Small, lightweight watering can and water
- Snack (optional)

Opening Ceremony: Hello Around the World (Mexico and Spain) and the Girl Scout Promise

Have the girls gather in a Daisy Circle. Let them know that today they will say hello to one another in Spanish, a language known by Cora, one of the main characters in the story of Amazing Daisy. Explain that in Spanish, which is spoken in many countries, including Mexico and Spain, people say hello by saying, *"¡Hola!"* which sounds like *Ola*. Going around the circle, ask each girl to say "*Hola*" to the girl to her left. Once the girls have completed the circle, ask them to join you in saying the Girl Scout Promise:

> *On my honor, I will try:*
>> *To serve God and my country,*
>> *To help people at all times,*
>> *And to live by the Girl Scout Law.*

Learning the Girl Scout Sign

Next, explain to the girls that today they will learn the Girl Scout sign. Explain that the sign is the way Girl Scouts greet each other around the world—a silent kind of Girl Scout "hello." Show the sign to them in detail, demonstrating it with your own hand so all the girls can see. Explain how the three fingers held straight up represent the three parts of the Girl Scout Promise that they just said out loud together.

Then, ask girls to pair up while still remaining loosely in their Daisy Circle. Ask each pair of girls to make the Girl Scout sign to each other. Move around the circle to see if any girls need assistance with forming the sign. Consider linking your own actions to the Girl Scout Law; explain to the girls that by looking to see if any of them need assistance, you are being *friendly and helpful*, and that's a key Girl Scout value. Point to that line on your "big version" of the Girl Scout Law, and perhaps even suggest that second-year Daisies take a turn at being friendly and helpful by assisting younger girls in the group. When all girls have successfully made the Girl Scout sign, *congratulate* them on learning another Girl Scout tradition.

Mini-Garden Watering Time

Have the girls join with their planting partner (from Session 1) and then have each pair of girls *lightly* water their part of the group's mini-garden. (Remember: With basil, *warm* water really counts.)

- Emphasize that by watering their plantings the girls are caring for them and nurturing them—they're being responsible for them, and that's a key Girl Scout value.

- You might even point to the "responsible for what I say and do" line of the Law (on your big version) for emphasis.

- If any seeds have sprouted, note how well the girls' garden project is going. If nothing has sprouted, remind the girls that it takes time for seeds to sprout, that gardening requires some waiting time—and what adults call "patience."

Garden Story Time

Ask the girls to sit in their Daisy Circle so you can read them the next chapter of the Amazing Daisy story. Before you start, encourage the girls to volunteer anything they remember from the story. If the girls have trouble recalling the story, start to give them a brief summary and they will likely chime in with what they remember. If necessary, remind them of the story's three girls and how they walked home from school one day, saw one pretty daisy in the old garden, and then fell asleep. Then begin reading Chapter 2.

With the girls still in their Daisy Circle, explore the three questions that follow Chapter 2:

- Do you have any keys? (If the girls do have keys, ask them what they unlock. The girls may not yet have house keys, but they could have a key to a special box or lock.)

- How many keys does your family use?

- Where does your family keep its keys?

Consider first talking about (and even showing) the number of keys you carry each day. Then encourage the girls themselves to talk about keys. If no girls have keys and they aren't sure what keys their family uses, ask them what keys they hope to someday carry with them when they are older.

After the discussion, explain that it's time to get up and move around—and have some more fun with garden animals.

FUN FACTS ALONG THE GARDEN PATH

Chapters 2 through 5 of the Amazing Daisy story are sprinkled with fun facts related to the story's many characters that will spark the girls' interest in gardens, flowers, larger botanical and global issues, and the environment.

While reading the story to the girls, feel free to pause to talk with them about any of these factoids—or stick to the story and tell them some of the fun facts after they've heard the full chapter.

Garden Scamper

Have the girls create two lines in a large, open space. Explain that you will call out the name of a garden critter, such as rabbit, bird, or grasshopper. The two girls at the far end of the line must run up through the center of the two lines together by using the movements of that critter. (For a bird, the girls would flap their arms while running; for a rabbit, they would hop across the room.) Once the girls arrive at the top of the line, they can decide on a critter to call out, and the two girls standing at the far end of the line must now run up the middle, imitating the critter the two "callers" chose. Continue through the line of girls until all have called out a critter and all have run up the line.

Closing Ceremony: Friendship Squeeze

Ask the girls to come together again in a Daisy Circle. If they've chosen their own closing ceremony, suggest that they perform it. Otherwise, explain that they will now join hands, as they did at their last gathering, for the special Girl Scout closing ceremony called the friendship squeeze. Ask the girls if they remember how they held hands last time. If not, show them again (or better yet, ask a second-year Daisy to show them).

Then, thank the girls for another great Daisy Girl Scout gathering. Encourage them to share their book with their families, and let them know you look forward to the group's next time together.

"**The love of gardening** is a seed that once sown never dies, but always grows and grows to an enduring and ever-increasing source of happiness."

—Gertrude Jekyll, garden designer and author, 1843–1932, from *Wood and Garden*

SAMPLE SESSION 3
Greetings and Friendship

AT A GLANCE

Goal: Girls deepen their understanding of the Girl Scout Law, particularly the fifth value, "being responsible for what I say and do."

- Opening Ceremony: Hello Around the World (France and Parts of Africa), Girl Scout Sign and Promise
- Girl Scout Handshake
- Mini-Garden Watering Time
- Garden Story Time

- Reviewing the Girl Scout Law
- Imitating Nature
- Snack (optional)
- Closing Ceremony: Earning the Watering Can Award

MATERIALS

- Girls' book and this guide
- Poster board with Girl Scout Promise (from Session 1) or Promise written on whiteboard/chalkboard
- The girls' mini-garden

- Small, lightweight watering can and water
- Snack (optional)

Opening Ceremony: Hello Around the World (France and Parts of Africa), Girl Scout Sign and Promise

Continue the tradition of forming a Daisy Circle and saying hello in a new language. In this session, greet the girls with *bonjour*, and explain that it is the word for hello in French. Let the girls know that French is a language spoken in France and also in several African countries, including Cameroon, Madagascar, Mali, Morocco, and Rwanda. Explain to the girls that today, when they hear more of the Daisy story, they will meet a new flower named Mari. Explain that Mari is from Africa and also has family in France, so *bonjour* is a word that Mari would know well.

After all the girls have said *bonjour*, greet them with the Girl Scout sign and ask them to pair up and greet each other with the sign, too. Then, ask the girls to join together to recite the Girl Scout Promise. (The large, handwritten copy of the Promise that you used in Session 1 can continue to serve as a handy visual reference for the girls.)

Girl Scout Handshake

Next, explain to the girls that today they will learn another Girl Scout tradition: the Girl Scout handshake. Let them know that the handshake is the way Girl Scouts greet each other all around the world. Show the girls how the Girl Scout handshake is made by shaking with your left hand while making the Girl Scout sign with your right hand. If you have any second-year Daisies in your group, ask them to demonstrate the Girl Scout handshake for the whole group.

Explain to the girls that the left-handed handshake—in contrast to the right-handed handshake that most people use—represents friendship, because the left hand is closer to the heart than the right.

Ask all the girls to pair up around the Daisy Circle and have each pair of girls greet each other with the Girl Scout handshake.

When all the pairs of girls have shaken hands, congratulate them on learning another important Girl Scout tradition.

Mini-Garden Watering Time

As in Session 2, have the girls join with their planting partners and then have each pair of girls *lightly* water their part of the group's mini-garden—with *warm* water if growing basil. Have them check for any new growth. If nothing has popped up, again remind the girls that it can take several weeks for seeds to sprout (especially citrus seeds). Remind them that gardening requires *patience*, but their watering is still very important. They're caring for the seeds and being responsible for them—and those are values important to Girl Scouting, just like the Girl Scout Law says.

BEST BASIL: PLUCK SMART, WATER LIGHT

Once their basil plants produce several sets of leaves, show the girls how the leaves grow in pairs, one set above the other. To keep the plant branching well, have the girls pluck (and eat) the plant's top leaves. The leaf buds directly below will form a new set of branches. It's important to pluck the top leaves continually to prevent the plant from flowering. Once basil flowers, it's done growing and will be headed on a downward spiral. Overwatering will also hurt a basil plant beyond repair. So at each session, encourage smart plucking and light watering.

FOR LETTUCE LOVERS

Adults who planted lettuce as children often recall the great fun and wonder of plucking (and eating) outer leaves as the plant continued to grow. Baby lettuces and microgreens are now incredibly popular, so encourage the girls to pluck and taste while their plants are young.

"He who plants a garden plants happiness."

—Chinese proverb

Garden Story Time

Gather the girls into a Daisy Circle to read them Chapter 3 of the Amazing Daisy story. Before you start, ask if they remember what happened in Chapter 2. Allow time for any girls to talk about any scenes or characters that they remember and like. If necessary, offer a simple summary, such as: "The three girls, Chandra, Campbell, and Cora, woke up and found themselves locked in the garden. But a little bee helped them, and led them to dig up an old tin box. In that box, they found a letter from Daisy Gordon Low, and a key to the garden gate."

Now that you've read Chapter 3 to the girls, explore with them some of the characteristics of the flowers. Sunny, for example, is friendly and helpful. Ask the girls questions like:

- Can anyone think of another word for friendly? (If girls don't respond quickly, suggest your own answers, such as "nice," "kind," etc., and give an example of when you have been friendly. Then pose some situations for the girls. You might ask, for example, "If you meet a new girl at school and you invite her to lunch, are you being friendly?" Or "How about if you see the new girl sitting alone at recess. If you ask to play with her, are you being friendly?"

Try some similar questioning with the word *helpful*. Perhaps give an example of when you have been helpful recently and then ask the girls to think of something they do at home that is helpful for their families.

Guide the girls through similar questions using the characters of Zinni, who is considerate and caring, and Mari, who is responsible for what she says and does. You might let the girls know that Zinni, like all zinnias, has lots of leaves—a good characteristic for a flower that is considerate and caring. The girls might think of her many leaves as many caring hands. And Mari, being a marigold, is one of the most responsible flowers in the garden. Marigolds are known for keeping garden pests in check. As always, aim to engage all girls in the discussion.

OF MARIGOLDS AND FAMILY TREES

If the girls show interest in the diversity of the flower characters, you might offer up some simple flower facts to supplement those already in their book. You could explain, for example, that Mari, who was born in Africa, can trace her family roots back to Central America and Mexico. Where do the Daisies in your group trace their roots to?

Reviewing the Girl Scout Law

Explain to the girls that by learning about Sunny, Zinni, and Mari, they have also started learning about one of the most important parts of Girl Scouting: the Girl Scout Law.

Say just the first lines of the Girl Scout Law:

> *I will do my best to be*
> *honest and fair,*
> *friendly and helpful,*
> *considerate and caring,*

Explain how two of those lines match up to the characters of Sunny and Zinni:

• Sunny is friendly and helpful.

• Zinni is considerate and caring.

Ask the girls if they can think of other ways to be friendly and helpful or considerate and caring. Then read the full Law to the girls:

> *I will do my best to be*
> *honest and fair,*
> *friendly and helpful,*
> *considerate and caring,*
> *courageous and strong, and*
> *responsible for what I say and do,*
> *and to*
> *respect myself and others,*
> *respect authority,*
> *use resources wisely,*
> *make the world a better place, and*
> *be a sister to every Girl Scout.*

Explain to the girls how another flower, Mari, also matches up to a line from the Girl Scout Law:

• Mari is responsible for what she says and does.

Ask the girls if they know what it means to be responsible for what they say and do. Can they give examples of being responsible? (Remind them of their mini-garden.)

Let the girls know that as they continue to hear the story of Amazing Daisy and the Daisy Flower Garden, they will meet more flowers that match the rest of the values in the Girl Scout Law that they have just heard.

Imitating Nature

While the girls are still in their Daisy Circle, talk to them about how natural objects appear in the outdoors. Ask the girls to name some natural objects that they have seen outdoors. Then, going around the Daisy Circle, ask each girl to tell something about a natural object—grass, rocks, or trees, for example. If they have trouble talking about a natural object, gently prompt them with questions like: "How about grass? Is grass hard or soft? What color is grass?" Then, once you have gone around the circle, explain that you are going to name a natural object, and you want all the girls to pretend to be that object.

- Explain that when you name an object, you'd like the girls to position their bodies just like that object, and to move about like that object.

- Name various natural objects, one after the other, such as a tree, a rock, a blade of grass, a soft cloud, the warm sun, a butterfly, an ant, a worm, a bird, or any other object of your choice. Aim to keep the choices related to the area where the girls live (if they live in the Southwest, for example, you might ask them to pretend to be a cactus).

- If you think the girls are up for the challenge, ask them to take turns pretending to be an object—instead of acting as a group—and have the other girls guess what each girl is pretending to be.

Closing Ceremony: Earning the Watering Can Award

Explain to girls that being responsible for their mini-garden and deepening their understanding of the Girl Scout Law has earned them their first leadership award, the Daisy Watering Can. To celebrate, consider a festive ceremony of songs, poems, and/or garden skits—perhaps in conjunction with the session's mini-garden watering time. Aim for songs that reflect the Girl Scout Law, such as "I Will Do My Best" by NancyJean Tripp and Sue Stitt:

I Will Do My Best

I will do my best to be honest.
I will do my best to be fair.
I will do my best through my words
and my deeds to show
how much I really care.

Chorus:

I'm just one girl in this great wide
world, I can't go on every quest.
But I will do all I can do, and I will
do my best.

I will do my best to be a sister,
to each and every Girl Scout;
to observe, conserve, and preserve
the natural wonders all about.

Chorus

I will do my best to be wherever,
I am needed to be.
To live by the Law and my Promise
but most of all to always be me.

Chorus

Young children love the rhyming fun of poetry, so consider rounding out the awards ceremony with a garden-related poem, especially one that mentions growing or watering:

The Oak and the Rose
by Shel Silverstein

An oak tree and a rosebush grew,
Young and green together,
Talking the talk of growing things—
Wind and water and weather.
And while the rosebush sweetly bloomed
The oak tree grew so high
That now it spoke of newer things—
Eagles, mountain peaks and sky.
"I guess you think you're pretty great,"
The rose was heard to cry,
Screaming as loud as it possibly could
To the treetop in the sky.
"And you have no time for flower talk,
Now that you've grown so tall."
"It's not so much that I've grown," said the tree,
"It's just that you've stayed so small."

After the girls receive their awards, encourage them to continue thinking about planting and growing. Explain that soon they will be able to join together and move from their mini-garden to a big garden in their community.

"A garden is a grand teacher. It teaches patience and careful watchfulness; it teaches industry and thrift; above all it teaches entire trust."

—Gertrude Jekyll, garden designer and author
(including *Gardens and Children*), 1843–1932

Preparing for Session 4

Clues and Lists

The active time in Session 4 calls for you to have on hand lists of clues that describe various items commonly found in gardens in your community, such as a tree, flower, birdbath, or birdhouse. Here's an example of a list of clues for a tree:

> I'M TALL. I GROW IN THE EARTH. MY TOP IS GREEN. MY BOTTOM IS OFTEN BROWN. I HAVE BRANCHES. I HAVE LEAVES. SOMETIMES I HAVE FLOWERS. CHILDREN CLIMB ME. WHAT AM I?

Prepare clues like these for several objects and have them on hand as notes to use when playing the Garden Clues game.

Also, for Session 4, think about the gardens and open spaces in your community. Consider using the Daisy Friends and Family Network to create a list of these garden assets: school gardens, town/city gardens, gardens at hospitals and nursing homes, Girl Scout properties with gardens, playgrounds with gardens. Using the Project Possibilities Lists that your Daisy network provided, consider which community areas might benefit from some simple beautification (a planting/growing gift, such as an indoor herb garden or easily maintained primrose plantings for a nursing home), and which areas might benefit from larger, more sustained care (such as gifts of compost or ladybugs for an outdoor community garden).

In Session 4, after you read the girls Chapter 4 of the Daisy story, use these lists of community spaces to stimulate the girls to think about how they might follow through on some of the flowers' needs that they just heard about in the story. Let them know that even though they are young, they can still think about, and then actually help, a garden space in their community.

Following the Daisy story, the girls may naturally gravitate to worm composting or ladybug growing. These are certainly two of the most beneficial gifts the girls could give to a garden.

Worm Composting Is Simple and Quick

This tidy method of turning kitchen scraps into nutrient-rich humus has probably been around as long as there have been worms. Once you have some worms and a box (and food scraps for the worms to eat), the worms just do their thing. At a comfy temperature, worms lay cocoons that hatch with two or more babies in a few weeks. So if you start with just 10 worms, you may have 1,500 worms in six months.

Consider having a Girl Scout Junior serve as Worm Compost Leader, guiding the Daisies through each step of the worm box-making and composting process. Worm composting boxes can be purchased, but they are also easily made out of plastic storage bins or wood. Directions are readily available on the Internet and basically follow this order:

• Boxes require air holes on top.

• Then in go the worms, and atop the worms a handful or so of soil (grit to help the worms break down their food).

• Then comes the food (kitchen waste such as corn cobs, apple cores, wilted lettuce, coffee grounds, even tea bags and small amounts of cheese (but no meat), and then a top layer of "bedding"—damp, shredded black-and-white newspaper.

• The box is then closed and the worms are left to wiggle in peace.

Over the weeks and months, as the food decomposes and more food and bedding are added, both food and paper are eaten by the worms, which send it all back out as worm castings (a polite term for worm excrement). The castings, which smell like fresh earth and are rich in nitrogen, phosphorus, and potassium, make a nice, organic fertilizer. When mixed with equal parts of potting soil and water-absorbing vermiculite or sand, castings make perfect plant soil. Or they can be placed alone atop the soil around plants, as a "top dressing."

Ladybugs Offer Pest Protection, Beauty, Fascinating Facts

Ladybugs love to eat aphids, those tiny green garden pests that suck the sap from plants. Ladybugs can be purchased full grown by mail, and it can be exciting for children to receive a package, peek inside, and then release these beautiful and beneficial insects into a garden. But growing the bugs will likely be more rewarding (don't miss the last funny fact here):

• Ladybugs grow from larvae to adult in two to three weeks.

• As larvae, ladybugs look like little alligators.

• Their spots appear about 12 hours after hatching.

• A ladybug will eat 5,000 aphids in its lifetime.

• Ladybugs live for one year (and hibernate during winter).

• When ladybugs sense danger, they roll over and play dead.

KEEP THAT GARDEN GROWING

Want to spread your Daisies' garden journey over more than one season, so the girls discover the cycles of nature? Consider engaging your group of Daisies in both fall and spring growing projects. An indoor planting of lettuces or herbs in fall might be followed by bulb or flower plantings for spring.

"The most noteworthy thing about gardeners is that they are always optimistic, always enterprising . . . They always look forward to doing something better than they have ever done before."

—Vita Sackville-West, poet, novelist, and gardener, 1892–1962

SAMPLE SESSION 4

Good Thoughts, Good Deeds, Garden Needs

AT A GLANCE

Goal: Girls deepen their understanding of the Girl Scout Law, particularly the fifth value, "being responsible for what I say and do."

- Opening Ceremony: Hello Around the World (The Netherlands and Iran) and Girl Scout Promise
- Garden Story Time
- Take Action Project Brainstorm

- Mini-Garden Watering Time
- What's in the Bag
- Snack
- Closing Ceremony

MATERIALS

- Girls' book and this guide
- Poster board with Girl Scout Promise (from Session 1) or Promise written on whiteboard/chalkboard
- The girls' mini-garden (plus watering can and water)
- Paper bag

- Selection of items found in nature, depending on your location: rocks, stones, twigs, shells, pieces of bark, pine cones, acorns or other large seeds or seed pods
- Blindfold
- Snack (optional)
- The girls' mini-garden

Opening Ceremony: Hello Around the World (The Netherlands and Iran) and Girl Scout Promise

Continue the fun tradition of forming a Daisy Circle and saying hello in a new language. Once the girls are in their circle, ask them if they know another way of saying "hello." Then, greet them with *hallo*, explaining that it is the word for hello in Dutch, which is spoken in the Netherlands, home of Tula, the tulip. Remind the girls that they met Tula in Chapter 4 of the Daisy story, and that Tula is from the Netherlands but her family is originally from Iran. Explain that in Iran, people use the word *salam* to say hello. So both *hallo* and *salam* are words that Tula might know well.

- Ask the girls to go around the circle saying either *hallo* or *salam* to each other (their choice).

- Then have them pair up and greet each other with the Girl Scout sign.

- As in Session 3, ask the girls to get back into their Daisy Circle and join together to recite the Girl Scout Promise. (And let them see your poster board/whiteboard/chalkboard version of the Promise—by now it may be a nice, reassuring message for them.)

Garden Story Time

Let the girls know that it's now time to hear more of the story of Amazing Daisy, so they'll want to get comfortable!

Take Action Project Brainstorm

After reading them Chapter 4, and with the girls still sitting in their Daisy Circle, ask them what *they* would do to help the flowers.

- If your group of girls is already growing basil, would they want to bring some basil to the garden?

- Would they want to bring worms?

- Ladybugs?

Encourage all the girls to join in the discussion.

Next, ask the girls if they noticed how the newest flower friends in the story connect to the Girl Scout Law. Guide them through all or some of the new characters:

- Lupe, the light blue lupine, is honest and fair.

- Tula, the red tulip, is courageous and strong.

- Gloria, the purple morning glory, respects herself and others.

- Gerri, the magenta geranium, respects authority.

- Clover knows how to use resources wisely.

- Vi, the violet, is a sister to every Girl Scout.

- Rosie, the rose, makes the world a better place.

You might give examples of your own behavior (perhaps something that happened on the way to meeting the Daisies today) and relate it to one of the flowers' Law values. Then offer more examples of similar behavior and ask the girls to name which Law value that behavior represents.

When you have a good discussion going, guide the girls to the character of Rosie, who makes the world a better place. A great goal here would be to get the girls thinking again of how Cora, Campbell, and Chandra are trying to help the Daisy Flower Garden. See if your group of Girl Scout Daisies can agree on a garden project they all find fun and interesting. (Use the Daisy network's Project Possibilities lists to jumpstart the girls' ideas.) It's likely that girls at this age are interested in everything: growing things, raising pretty ladybugs, having some fun with wiggly worms. So next, ask them to take these ideas—and any others they came up with—home with them. Talking with their parents or older siblings, they might get some more good ideas—and good feedback. Explain to the girls that after they get their families involved, they will then plan to help a garden in their own community—they will team up together for a community action project.

Mini Garden Watering Time

As the discussion wraps up, have the girls join with their planting partners and then lightly water their part of the group's mini-garden. (Don't forget to use warm water if growing basil.) Have the girls check for new growth. Remind them that their watering is very important to their garden's health. They're being responsible for their plants, and that's a nice start to living the Girl Scout Law.

What's in the Bag?

Let the girls know it's now time to have some fun with things that live in a garden. This game is a great way to heighten the sense of touch and practice language skills.

You'll need:

Paper bag

Blindfold (scarf or napkin)

Things found in nature: rocks, stones, twigs, shells, pieces of bark, pine cones (or cones from other evergreen trees), acorns or other large seeds or seed pods

- Place two to four items in the paper bag.

- Ask the girls to take turns picking one object from the bag while blindfolded. Have each girl, during her turn, describe how her object feels. Encourage her to use words such as smooth, rough, spiky, fuzzy, etc.

- Let each girl guess what her object is, then have her remove her blindfold to see if she guessed correctly.

Closing Ceremony

After a friendship squeeze, encourage the girls to share their gardening ideas with their families, and let them know that you look forward to the group's next time together—when they will all move ahead with their big garden plan.

Preparing for Session 5 and Beyond

You and your Daisy crew will choose how you gather for Sessions 5 and 6—and possibly a separate celebratory closing. Your choices will be based on:

The Daisies' Take Action Project

Whether the girls' project is large or small and various practicalities (location, which friends/family will help transport Daisies, the date and time, etc.).

The Daisies' Garden Party

As with the Take Action Project, the girls' celebration can be large or small, simple or all-out.

You can easily see how this journey might grow to more than six sessions—possibly even 10—giving girls plenty of time to take action and also plan and create their garden party. But don't worry; if you really need to complete the journey in six sessions, just follow the basic framework for Sessions 5 and 6 given in this guide. All you need to do is add in the particulars of the girls' Take Action Project and anything that might make their garden party truly fabulous.

"**Half the interest** of a garden is the constant exercise of the imagination."

—Mrs. C. W. (Maria Theresa) Earle, horticulturist and gardener, 1836–1925, from *Pot-Pourri from a Surrey Garden*

SAMPLE SESSION 5
Doing and Growing

AT A GLANCE

Goal: Girls achieve success with their plant/grow Take Action Project. (Activities may vary depending on the girls' project and whether they are "on location" or at their "home base.")

- Opening Ceremony: Hello Around the World (Japan) and Girl Scout Promise
- Garden Story Time
- Mini-Garden Watering Time
- Secret Garden Stuff
- Snack (optional)
- Closing Ceremony: Earning the Golden Honey Bee Award

MATERIALS

- Girls' book and this guide
- Poster board with Girl Scout Promise (from Session 1) or Promise written on whiteboard/chalkboard
- The girls' mini-garden (plus watering can and water)
- Golden Honey Bee Awards
- Snack (optional)

Opening Ceremony: Hello Around the World (Japan) and Girl Scout Promise

Continue the fun tradition of forming a Daisy Circle and saying hello in a new language. Once the girls are in their circle, greet them with *konnichiwa*, explaining that it is the word for hello in Japanese. Explain to the girls that today, as they hear more of the Daisy story, they will meet Tamiko, a girl whose family is from Japan.

- Ask the girls to go around the circle saying either *konnichiwa* or one of the other ways to say hello that they have learned as Daisy Girl Scouts (their choice).

- Then have girls pair up and greet each other with the Girl Scout sign.

- Then, as in earlier sessions, ask the girls to form their Daisy Circle and join together to recite the Girl Scout Promise. By now, your poster board (or whiteboard/chalkboard) version of the Promise may not even be needed.

Garden Story Time

Ask the girls to sit in their Daisy Circle so you can read them the next chapter of the Amazing Daisy story. Before you start, ask the girls to help you remember what has happened in the story so far. If they can't, give a brief summary, reminding them of how Daisy's flower friends appeared in the garden and talked to the three girls about all their wishes and needs. Then begin reading Chapter 5.

Next, start a discussion with the girls about the details of the story they've just heard. Ask questions like:

- Have any of you ever seen a ladybug? What color was it? Did you hold it in your hand?

- Do you know what ladybugs are best known for?

- How about worms? Have any of you seen worms wriggling around after a rain?

- How would you like to have some worms to eat up your fruit and vegetable peelings so you wouldn't have any food to throw out in the garbage?

- If you could plan a garden party, what would you serve?

Remind the girls that Cora's mom said gardens are about choices. By now, many of the Daisies in your group will have created their own gardens in their book. Consider using this time to ask girls to share their garden "choices."

KEEP IT GIRL LED

No matter what route the girls take with their project, here are some pointers for keeping their Garden Party girl led:

- Have girls create festive garlands or hats (or another item of their choice) to wear during the party.

- Have girls invite family and friends to the party (if your group is large, consider limiting the number of guests per girl).

- Serve garden-related foods of the girls' choice.

Mini-Garden Watering Time

As the girls move ahead with their larger garden project, it's good to remind them that they are still caretakers of the mini-garden they planted at the start of their garden journey. So, unless the mini-garden has already become a gift to the community, follow the usual watering procedure.

Next, let the girls know it's now a good time to play an active game called Secret Garden Stuff:

SECRET GARDEN STUFF

The girls are divided into teams, and each team member is given a number. On signal, number ones from each team run to you (the adult volunteer), and you secretly show them a garden object.

The number ones then run back to their teams and describe the object as accurately as they can without naming it. When the team has decided what the object is, number ones return to you and tell you their answer. The first team to name the garden object correctly wins. For the next round, number twos come to you to look at a garden object, and so on through the entire set of girls.

Closing Ceremony: Earning the Golden Honey Bee Award

If girls have completed their Take Action Project, they now earn the Golden Honey Bee Award. Consider a festive ceremony with a bee "dance," a tribute to Honey, the buzzing bee in the Daisy story. Let girls know they have earned the Bee for their action to make the world a better place.

Preparing for Session 6 (and possibly beyond)

Session 6 represents a special time in Girl Scout Daisies' lives. They've planned a community garden project and are on their way to putting it in place and being full-fledged stewards of the environment. That means it's nearing time for them to earn their Amazing Daisy Award and celebrate with a garden party.

Make the project's "unveiling" a central focus of the celebration. The unveiling can be a show-and-tell shared with family and friends, community members, other groups of Daisies in your area, or older Girl Scouts.

Let the girls do the "unveiling" by explaining to their guests what they did and why they chose to do it. Each girl might also say what she liked best about carrying out the project.

Then you might kick up the garden theme with some fun, funny, and inspiring garden poetry. Here are some samples:

The kiss of the sun for pardon,
The song of the birds for mirth,
One is nearer God's heart in a garden
Than anywhere else on earth.

—Dorothy Frances Gurney, from "God's Garden"

Life is like a garden
And friendship like a flower,
That blooms and grows in beauty
With the sunshine and the shower.

—Helen Steiner Rice, from "Friendship's Flower"

I will be the gladdest thing
Under the sun!
I will touch a hundred flowers
And not pick one.

—Edna St. Vincent Millay, from "Afternoon on a Hill"

You might also suggest that the girls sing or chant the Daisy song (it's on pages 5 and 21 of their book and the next page of this guide) or another song of their choice.

Sandy's Song for Girl Scout Daisies

Words and Music by Sandy Thomas

"The [person] who has planted a garden feels that [she] has done something for the good of the world."

—Charles Dudley Warner, American essayist and novelist, 1829-1900, from *My Summer in a Garden*

SAMPLE SESSION 6
Celebrating the Law with a Garden Party

AT A GLANCE

Goal: Girls understand the meaning of the Girl Scout Law and its role in their daily life.

Activities will vary depending on the garden project and "garden party path" chosen by your group of Girl Scout Daisies. Here are some suggestions:

- Opening Ceremony: Hello Around the World and Girl Scout Promise
- Garden Story Time
- A Note for Future Girl Scout Daisies
- Garden Project Unveiling
- Earning the Amazing Daisy Award
- Garden Party

Opening Ceremony

Have the girls gather in a Daisy Circle. Let them know that today they will say hello to each other in any language they choose from among those learned during their time on their garden journey. If the girls are up for it, add one twist: As girls go around the circle saying hello, no girl can repeat the same hello said by the girl who spoke just before her. Then invite any guests to step forward to say hello in a language of their choice.

Once all hellos are complete, ask the Girl Scout Daisies to join together to say the Girl Scout Promise.

Garden Story Time

Next, invite the girls (and any guests) to sit comfortably to hear the final chapter of the Daisy story.

A Note for Future Girl Scout Daisies

When the reading is done, ask the girls to join together to talk through their ideas for what's important for future Girl Scout Daisies—like Chandra, Campbell, and Cora did in the story. Capture the girls' ideas on paper so that you can make copies of them and present them to the girls to place in their book.

Next, perhaps ask the girls to share their favorite moment from the Daisy story.

Earning the Amazing Daisy Award

Next, bring the girls together to say the full Girl Scout Law. Then, let them know it's time for them to earn the Amazing Daisy Award. Let the girls and their guests know why the Daisies have earned it. You might say to the girls, "You've earned this Amazing Daisy Award because you've made the Promise to live the Law."

Garden Party

Once all awards are handed out, let the garden party begin!

GARDEN PROJECT UNVEILING

During this final journey session, the girls will unveil their garden project and explain it to their guests.

If the girls don't say it on their own, point out that through their project they've come to live the Girl Scout Law in various ways: They've been friendly and helpful, considerate and caring, and, of course, they've made the world a better place.

Depending on the girls' project and how they carried it out, other values of the Law may also apply to your group of Daisies.

Congratulations!